T0062852

MY ROAD TO RESURRECTION

SaavyGirl

BALBOA.
PRESS
A DIVISION OF HAY HOUSE

ISBN: 978-1-4525-5320-7 (sc)
ISBN: 978-1-4525-5321-4 (e)

Balboa Press books may be ordered through booksellers or by contacting:

Balboa Press
A Division of Hay House
1663 Liberty Drive
Bloomington, IN 47403
www.balboapress.com
1-(877) 407-4847

Because of the dynamic nature of the Internet, any web addresses or links contained in this book may have changed since publication and may no longer be valid. The views expressed in this work are solely those of the author and do not necessarily reflect the views of the publisher, and the publisher hereby disclaims any responsibility for them.

The author of this book does not dispense medical advice or prescribe the use of any technique as a form of treatment for physical, emotional, or medical problems without the advice of a physician, either directly or indirectly. The intent of the author is only to offer information of a general nature to help you in your quest for emotional and spiritual well-being. In the event you use any of the information in this book for yourself, which is your constitutional right, the author and the publisher assume no responsibility for your actions.

Any people depicted in stock imagery provided by Thinkstock are models, and such images are being used for illustrative purposes only.
Certain stock imagery © Thinkstock.

Printed in the United States of America

Balboa Press rev. date: 7/20/2012

DEDICATION

To my son:
*I love you. Always be happy, listen to your inner voice,
and follow the dreams you will soon believe in.*

To My family and friends:
*I want to thank you for all your continued love and support over the
years; I wouldn't be where I am without you.*

To the readers:
*We all have a past. I hope that you will read this story,
and know that you are not defined by your past,
but still in control to building a much brighter future.*

CONTENTS

My Happiest Memories

My earliest memory is from when I was about eleven or twelve. I have a distinct, vivid memory of myself in a pink-and-white dress and a pair of white sandals. My hair, parted in the middle, hung down my back in two braids. I remember that the clothes that I was wearing were new, and I was so happy to have them. I was anxious to show my friends my new white sandals. I remember thinking that I wasn't going to jump rope that day because I was wearing my new clothes. I remember smiling and being happy.

At that age, I was about five foot four and shy—a cute, chubby little girl. I loved jumping rope and doing cheers, just like most other girls my age. My older brother, Terrence, was one year older than me. My brother was a happy young boy, outgoing, who was well liked by most of his friends. He was dark-skinned and stood about five foot ten in height. When my brother and I were younger, we argued and fought like most siblings do, but as we'd grown up we had become very close, despite the fact that our personalities were very different. I was more like my father, who was more quiet and reserved. My brother, on the other hand, took on more of my mother's personality, more outspoken and to the point.

I grew up in a lower-class family in Brookside, New York, in the 1970s. My mother was a working woman who appeared to like her job. She surrounded herself with family and friends. My father, a popular guy, also had many friends at his job at the Sanitation Department. Summer was probably my favorite season, because during summer the neighborhood had many block parties. All the tenants of the block would get together and have barbecues and celebrate with food and music. Each area in Brookside had a particular day for its block party. When I was growing up, the neighborhood was a close-knit community; most of the people who lived in the area had lived there for many years and everyone knew everyone else's family.. The buildings in the community were several stories high and housed about fifty families each. It was more like one big extended family in that way.

My family's name on my mother's side is O'Neil. My grandmother, Vesta, had ten children, so my family was very well-known in the neighborhood. My grandmother had grown depressed after my grandfather died, and needed help raising her ten children. My mother was the second oldest girl, so she was expected to help out with the other children. Everyone in the neighborhood called my mother Deborah, but to family she was mostly just Debbi.

My mother was sassy, job-oriented, and very smart. I remember her being tall, thin, and very outgoing. My mother had a petite body and often wore stylish clothing. My mother was very popular in the neighborhood and had a good group of friends, even though she had to help out with taking care of the rest of the children. My mother did as she was told—but also had her fun too. My other aunts and uncles looked up to my mother because she helped to raise them when they were younger.

My father's family was called Simmons. The Simmonses were a small family. Ann, my paternal grandmother, had only one child, Marcus. As an only child, my father had a very different childhood than my mother. Still, my father had other family members in other parts of New York. My dad was medium height, handsome, and a party-goer who, as an only child, got his way most of the time.

My parents had a lot of friends in common, which is how they met. They were young teenagers when they first met, so they dated for many years before my brother and I came along. My mother became pregnant at the age of sixteen. I think my father wasn't ready to have a family, because he went into the military when my brother and I were still young. My mother was left alone with babies; I think that was very hard for her. Still, she tried to raise my brother and me the best she could with the help of family and friends. Many of her friends were family friends from her childhood, and were around my brother and me as we grew up.

My father spent a few years in the military and then returned home; my brother and I were already in school by then. My parents got back together and we moved into our first apartment in Brookside, on Market Street. We stayed there for a few years. Both of my parents luckily got city jobs at young ages. My mother worked for the Department of Corrections and my father worked for the Department of Sanitation. My brother and I attended Eatsville Elementary School until I was in the second grade.

BEFORE THE STORM

When I look back, I feel like we had a real family in the apartment on Market Street. I could remember my mother planning day-trips to places like Bear Mountain in Hudson Valley for the day. I used to get excited to go to Bear Mountain, because I knew that my mother was going to fry chicken and make macaroni salad, two of my favorite foods. We also went to Connecticut to Danbury State Fair, Prospect Park Zoo in Brooklyn, and Flushing Meadows Park in Queens. Remembering these trips makes me smile, because those memories remind me of the happiest moments of my childhood.

I used to go outside and sit on the steps of the building where we lived and talk with my friends. Sometimes, the other girls who lived on the block and I would jump rope—at the time, double dutch was very popular, and the other girls on Market Street and I could do all sorts of tricks and games. I loved it there..

One day my mother came home and told my brother and me that we were moving to Ocean Parkway. I didn't know how to feel; everything was great in my life and I was scared things would be different. I'm not really sure what prompted the move; maybe it was the area in which we lived, or it could have been the fact that we got robbed while out one night. Whatever the reason, I remember thinking two things: firstly, Ocean Parkway was going to be the worst place to live; and secondly, that my life would never be the same after we left our home in Brookside.

Still, although I knew things would change when we moved to Ocean Parkway, I never could have imagined how much. My first trip to see the new neighborhood was on the G train. The ride from Brookside to Ocean Parkway seemed so long that, to me, it felt like we had moved to another state. I'm sure it wasn't more than two hours, but it felt like forever. Eventually, the door buzzer rang and the train conductor announced, "Ocean Parkway." My mother and I rose and disembarked, and as we headed to the stairs, she took my hand.

The first time I saw the train station lobby, it was gloomy, dark, and cold. The doors along the side of the token booth were electric blue and silver. To the left of the token booth was a wooden block anchored to the cement floor with open-backed seats for waiting passengers. As I gazed around at the station, I couldn't help but hear the beeping signal that let passengers know a train was approaching the platform. Somehow, that beep remained my first impression of Ocean Parkway.

We walked off to see what my mother called our new home. It was about four blocks away from the train station. While we walked, I stayed quiet, thinking about the sights and sounds at the train station, wondering what our new home would be like.

I remember our new building being quite tall, tan, and in need of a good cleaning. Mom and I pulled open the doors and walked toward the elevator, just to the left of the mailboxes. I thought it was funny that the floors in the hallways were pale blue. The elevator rose slowly. Our new apartment was the last apartment on the left, seventh floor. Using her key to open the doo,r my mother walked inside; I followed. We stood still for a few minutes and took in the sizes and the layout: two moderately sized bedrooms, a bathroom, an eat-in kitchen, and a spacious living room. My parents' bedroom was across from the bathroom, and my brother's and my bedroom was between their room and the bathroom, to the side.

About a month later, we were moved in. By this time, my parents had been together for many years, maturing and growing into their parental roles. They were both dedicated to their jobs, so the longer commute didn't bother them. My brother and I started school at Ranker Elementary School in Queens. Since Terrence was outgoing and smart, he adjusted easily, but it wasn't quite the same for me. My shyness made it harder for me to make new friends so easily. We both did very well in school, though, and my brother always watched out for me so I never got into any trouble.

Adjusting to Change

We all slowly adjusted to our new area and surroundings. Of cousre, the adjustment was harder on some of us than others; it turned out that, in the end, it was harder on my parents than on their children.

After living in Ocean Parkway for about a year or so, my parents started doing drugs. Sometimes my brother and I would come home from school and see marijuana on the glass living room table. This was a new and unfamiliar area for my parents, so they spent most of their time together at first. Eventually, though, my father started to hang out more with his work friends. Sometimes my mother would watch from the kitchen window to see if my father was walking home from the train station. After a while, she grew tired of waiting and wanted to hang out with her own friends—and so that's what she started to do. My mother started bringing around people that she had met. She would introduce male and female friends to Terrence and me. She also started to stay out a lot.

The dynamic between my parents changed very quickly. Sometimes one of them would be home with my brother and me; then at other times neither of them would be there. When my father was home, he would get upset that my mother wasn't home. He would look for her and ask my brother and me where she had gone. We never knew, so that just added to my father's frustration. He eventually went out on his own to search for her, and then the two of them would argue. Sometimes the arguments got loud enough that my brother and I could hear what was being said, but we eventually got used to it. Over the next few months, it appeared that each of them wanted to do things their own way, and so they did. They took turns having their time to hang out with their friends while my brother and I stayed home alone to fend for ourselves. We were getting older, so we were better at taking care of ourselves anyway.

Sometimes, after my parents had spent a day out with friends, one of them would come home to rest to see if the other was home yet. Eventually my mother started to hang out much more than my father, and that appeared to be a big problem for him. At times my mother wanted to go out and my father wanted her to stay home. When she didn't stay, my father started to beat her. My brother and I used to sit in our bedroom and listen as my mother got hit over and over and over again. Sometimes she cried, but it almost didn't matter, because my father didn't stop the beatings whether she cried or not.
As children we were very upset and confused why he would beat our mother; we didn't really understand why it was happening in the first place. Eventually we started to resent our father for beating our mother repeatedly. I could feel myself growing cold against him for inflicting pain on her. I remember carrying this helpless feeling of hurt in my heart as the sounds of the beatings got louder with each blow. Terrence and I sat and talked quietly about hurting our father for what he used to do to our mother if we ever got the chance. There was little to nothing that we could do then, however, so we endured the day-to-day living as we knew it.

I think my mother saw how hurt my brother and I were, so she started to send us to visit family members for the weekends. On one hand this was a good thing, but on the other it made me worry more about my mother's safety. Still, we were glad to get a break from seeing and hearing the fights, so my brother and I started to look forward to the weekends. When it was time to return home, we were never sure about what we would be walking into, so we always entered the apartment with caution.

One day it became very obvious why we needed to be so careful. I came back from our grandmother's house in Brookside one day to find our parents fighting. Standing helpless on the side, I saw my mother run out of the bedroom to the hallway to get away from my father. My father ran after her and chased her in a fit of rage. Fearing for my mother's safety, I watched them out in the hallway, yelling at the top of their lungs at each other. On this occasion my brother hadn't gotten home yet, so I was even more scared. I peeked out into the hallway—and saw my father push my mother down a flight of stairs.

That night my mother was admitted to Thompson Hospital with multiple bruises and three broken ribs. The cops were called to speak with her about the incident that had resulted in her being treated in the emergency room. When they arrived they talked about pressing charges against my father, but she didn't do it. Before this incident I had no idea of that domestic violence had a name, but I learned and realized exactly what it meant. I had heard about it before, but up until now it was something that happened to other women.

After the hospital released my mother, we went back home as though nothing happened at all. My mother didn't speak of it, and neither did I. A few days later my father came home and saw the bruises he'd given my mother. This time it was too much for him to bear, so he decided it was time for him to leave. And he did.

My mother tried to pick up the pieces of moving on without him. She tried to take care of my brother and me as well as herself, but I could see that she wasn't happy alone. At some point I believe she grew resentful of the fact that my father had left her alone to raise two children on her own. She tried her best for a while, but I believe heartache got the best of her. She didn't really have any family support in the area, nor many friends in Ocean Parkway, so she turned to drugs.

When my mother's drug use increased, she left my brother and me home alone a lot more often. She continued to work, but then she'd go out partying, and eventually her using became much heavier. She was high most of the time. She managed to juggle her using with work, but not long after my father left, she lost her job at the Department of Corrections because she tested positive.

After my mother lost her job, she started spending a lot of time at home. Although I didn't know the words for it at the time, she fell into a heavily depressed state. This eventually changed after a few months, particularly as she started to spend more time getting high. There were times that my brother and I would come home to find complete strangers in our apartment, getting high with our mother. We just endured it as well as could be expected.

After about six months or so my father returned home; my parents had talked, and they said they were going to work things out. And for a while, they did; the arguing was down to very little. But, as the old saying goes, nothing lasts forever—and it was no different with my parents' relationship. The arguing and fighting started back up again after my father had been home for a few weeks. He started to beat my mother when she wanted to go out alone. My brother and I accepted this as normal, just as we had in the past. My father realized at some point that beating her up wasn't going to make my mother stop wanting to go out, and it didn't, so he finally stopped the abuse. He would make an effort to come home at night after work while my mother hung out. Somehow their roles had reversed.

I tried to cope by tuning it out and pretending I was ok. I stayed in my bedroom a lot, not going outside because I was shy and didn't have many friends at the time. Even though we had been settled for a while, the move was still very tough for me. I tried to cope the best I could, but the arguing and fighting made life more difficult to bear.

LIES AND DECEIT

In fifth grade, I slowly took an interest in making friends, but only a few. I still spent a lot of time at home in my room alone. My father started to spend a lot of time at home alone too, because my mother wanted to hang out with her friends. There were times I thought he was looking at me strangely, but never could I have imagined what was to come next.

My father started to want to be closer to me than he had before: sitting next to me on the couch, coming up behind me in the kitchen, things of that nature. Then the sexual touching started. I remember he would call me into his bedroom and whisper to me in a low voice to be quiet so that no one could hear what he was saying or doing. Because I was still young, I didn't understand what was happening; I only knew how nasty it made me feel when he touched me. I remember it being around the time I was learning about body parts and sex in my school, and eventually I figured out what was happening to me. I hated my father for doing that to me, and I hated myself for doing those things with him.

After I realized what was really happening, I started to hate myself. I began feeling worthless. When I thought about it, I said to myself that I couldn't believe that my own father ws doing this to me. I began to feel ashamed of myself. All I remember thinking is that I was this nasty girl doing things with my father, and no one would ever want me.

13

I was so grossly mortified that what I had learned about in school had become my worst nightmare at home. I felt dirty, guilty, and ashamed, but I didn't know what to do to make my father stop.

Making matters worse, I didn't feel like I could tell anyone what was going on or how I felt. I often thought of how I would tell someone what was happening, but days and even weeks went by without a word to anyone. At one point I remember wondering how you could make someone understand something that's happening to you when you don't even understand it yourself. Out of shame and probably fear, I stayed quiet with this dirty little secret for many months. I wanted to tell my mother, but I had mixed feelings because I didn't know if she would believe me.

Finally, after suffering in silence, I took a chance. One day while we were visiting my grandmother in Brookside, I blurted out everything that had happened. Neither one of us wanted to talk about it because it was uncomfortable—uncomfortable for me to tell her about it, and uncomfortable for her to hear that the guy she loved was molesting her daughter. I remember feeling relieved after telling the secret, but I knew deep down that things in my family would never be the same.

I eventually tried going back to living a normal child's life again after telling what happened, but I remember being depressed for most of the time. Even though the incest stopped once I had told my mother,— she must have confronted my father, although I didn't see her do it—I felt like the memories of it would never let me forget.

Tearing a Family Apart

Eventually the news of what my father had done traveled throughout the family. Some family members were supportive, while others made me out to be a liar. In my mind it was hard enough dealing with what had happened to me, but to have family members believe I was lying was almost too much to bear.

One of the people who chose to believe I was lying was my father's mother. She couldn't fathom that her only child would do such a thing. Also, my father was not honest with everyone; when my mother confronted him about what was happening, he denied it. Still, somehow I was shocked that he never told his own mother the truth. At that point, simply put, my grandmother decided to have little to nothing to do with me, and the relationship between us would forever be tainted. A distance between us had always existed in a weird way, but this situation just made it worse.

There were a lot of mixed feelings between my mother's and my father's family. I hated that I was made out to be a liar, which is what I had always feared would happen. Much of the family, particularly on my father's side, thought I was lying, evil, and manipulative. As others in the family distanced themselves from me, I was not merely hurt; I also felt like the incest was my fault. I had known that if I came forward, there would be changes in my life, but I really didn't think my father would deny it—maybe I was naïve about that. In fact, I had thought that when I told my mother about it, my father would apologize, tell his mother about what he did, and promise to never do it again. I even thought my mother would leave my father and choose me over him, that she would go to the police and report the incest, and that my father would go to jail. Sadly, the only thing that did happen was my father's departure—the incest stopped, life went on.

Afterward, I thought my life would go back to normal. However, I had this weird sense that merely by talking to me, people would be able to tell that I had been an incest victim. So, out of fear, I just chose not to make friends. In some ways I was in denial about dealing with what had happened; my mother and I had not talked about it since I told her. I didn't have anyone to talk to about how I was feeling. So over the next few years I coped by blocking it out. I never thought about how the incest affected my life until one day I looked back and wondered where my life had gone.

My denial lasted several years. Life moved on, and yet I was stuck in the past. I really didn't know how to express what I felt about the incest and the destruction of my family. It was as though I'd been walking along a road, when suddenly I was hit by a car and both of my legs were broken. When something like that happens, the victim goes into shock. When the initial shock wears off, the victim usually has the will to heal from the accident, but may also feel lost as to how they will continue the rest of their life. I feel like I got lost somewhere between the shock of the incest and how to heal fully after it stopped.

I never went to see anyone for counseling. I'm sure I could come up with a million reasons why I felt stuck in denial, but the fact of the matter is that I stayed there for far too long. When the incest stopped, I struggled emotionally, although I tried not to let on to anyone about my fragile emotional state. I struggled to live with what happened to me and my family. Even though the denial was hard, the pain of knowing what incest did to my family as a result for the incest was much more to endure. My mother would say to me that she never knew what was going on. My brother never commented on the matter; I don't believe he knew what to say either. I really felt the lack of my grandmother's love. In the end, I felt immense guilt, as though I had caused my family to fall apart.

Trying to pick up the pieces of my broken life, I became deeply depressed, bitter, and angry over the next few years. I carried around a lot of unaddressed pain and anger from the incest and its aftermath. Of course there were days when I did smile and even laugh, but I never forgot about how my life had changed. Now, I can admit that I developed an intense hate for men because of my experience with my own father. As a young lady, I didn't understand the root of my pain, nor did I know how I was going to move forward in my life. Lacking direction, I continued to carry around a great deal of pain, and then I realized that I also started to feel guilty.

Pain and Guilt

As I grew up, I continued to beat myself up for revealing the incest. I had known my life would change once I had told my mother about it, but never did I imagine how it would affect my feelings about myself. I felt guilty seeing the sadness in my mother's eyes after my father left. I know that she wanted the best for me and my brother, so she did what she had to do; it was also clear that she missed my father. My brother, who so easily adapted to new situations, now had to manage the loss of a father figure. I felt like it was entirely my fault.

I often longed for the family life we had before we moved to Ocean Parkway. I remember thinking if we had just stayed in Brookside, none of it would have happened. I also thought that maybe if I'd spoken up sooner, the incest wouldn't have affected my life so profoundly. Now that I'm older, I can say that I don't think anyone—unless an incest victim as well—really understands how incest affects a person's life. I felt guilty for the effect I thought I had had on my parents' relationship. On one hand, I know a lot of things played a part in breaking up my family unit; on the other, I couldn't help but think the part I played was huge.

I found myself analyzing what I could have done and said differently. I found myself in this very dark place with a huge cloud of guilt hanging over me. I found that the more I thought about my past, the more guilt I felt for the destruction of a family foundation. I can look back now and see the guilt I had for destroying my family was misplaced, but because I had little to no way of working through my problems, I couldn't see that at the time. With no one to talk to, I started to look to food to comfort me. I began to eat much more than necessary, using food to mask the underlying feelings of hurt and guilt.

Because the acts began around the time of puberty, I entered my teenage years with a twisted sense of what love from a man really was. I questioned the motives of every guy I ever dated. I developed a lack of trust in just about any male figure in my life, so I started dating, two, three, four guys at a time because I didn't feel like I could trust any of them. In my mid- teens, my mistrust and guilt turned to anger. I realized that I had lost respect for men; I couldn't fathom why, but I just knew how I felt. I did a lot of searching for love in the wrong places. I did not know then that the behavior I was displaying was abnormal; it was *my* normal. Now I know this is called "pent-up anger."

Only now, fifteen or more years later, can I articulate what I felt back then. Sometimes I question if my anger stemmed from the fact that my father molested me, or the fact that I grew up seeing my mother beaten and helpless, or the fact that no one ever thought to ask me about how I was doing. My parents weren't talkative; I was expected to move on as though things were okay. I tried this, but I began to fall apart at the seams. Of course things appeared fine on the outside, but clearly on the inside I was dying—or at least I thought I was. Things began to work themselves out in my behaviors and in my actions. I never told anyone this, but I started to skip school. There were days that my brother left for school and I would stay home alone; sometimes I just didn't care enough to get dressed. I can remember a few of my classmates asking me why I missed so much school. I really wanted to open up to the few friends that I had at the time, but the shame of my incest kept me in a dark, lonely hole. I cried very often. Most of the time I felt like I was alone, and would blame myself for what happened to my family practically every day. I could see and feel myself closing up like a lonely clam on a deserted beach.

As I got older I saw two things happening. I saw my brother enjoying his school years and getting closer with my father's side of the family. And I saw myself struggling through school, and growing more distant from living a happy life. At times I wouldn't talk to my brother because of how I felt. I knew he wasn't to blame; however, the happiness he brought back home after spending a weekend with my paternal grandmother often made me feel worse. Moreover, in a strange way I believed I deserved that pain.

I also felt angry about my body. I felt like I was ugly and fat. I tried many things to change the way I looked. I tried diets, pills, and just not eating all together. I got so angry at myself one time when the diet pills didn't make me lose weight fast enough. After that, I started staying outside more often during the day (which is when I found myself eating the most). This method worked for a while, but then I started to run into trouble with boys.

I met one guy when I was almost sixteen. He was my first true love, or so I thought. I stayed with him for a while, and I felt like I liked him a lot. I started to spend more time with him than with my family. Despite this, it took a long time for me to trust him. I remember I was always happy around him. Now I can say that it was temporary happiness because being with him got me out of the house; it kept me from being alone with my thoughts and guilt. Still, for the first time with a boy I didn't feel anger, sadness, shame, or guilt; instead, I saw a glimmer of sunshine. I really wanted to continue feeling like that, so over the next few years, attracting boys became the most important thing to me. For a while it had its perks: I received great gifts like expensive clothes, jewelry, flowers, and money. Sadly, none of those things took away the emotional worthlessness that I felt inside. When I went home, it was just me alone with my thoughts of inferiority. When I was alone, I realized that it was just me and this feeling of sadness, and no matter how many gifts I received my sadness had become a part of me. No matter what, it wasn't going away.

Stuck in a State of Denial

Life will move on with or without you. I constantly found myself knowing life was moving on, but I wasn't quite ready to go with it. I tried to do things like other teenagers my age. I had a few friends with whom I did enjoy spending time, but when I was with them I always questioned myself—I always thought someone would find out about the incest. Every day I pondered how I would handle it if someone found out. It made me sad that I couldn't enjoy being a normal teen with a normal life; I often cried when I saw other kids my age with parents who loved and cared for them.

I didn't realize how depressed I was until I was about seventeen. By this time I had moved out of my mother's house and into my grandmother's house. This change was very hard on me and saddened me deeply, because once again I was breaking up my family. Not only did I feel lost, but I felt like my world had fallen apart yet again. But at that time, many people thought this was the best solution me. Right now I can't say if it was the right thing to do or not. My mother was still doing drugs, and at times we had no food at home, and I was alone, too shy to go outside and face people. I had settled that this is how my life was going to be over the next few years, but In the middle of it a call was placed to ACS. Someone from ACS did come to my house and figured out what was happening, so, since I was a minor, I was removed from my mother's custody and sent back to live with relatives in Brookside.

Life didn't immediately improve during my stay at my grandmother's house. At first I stayed alone in my room a lot, but eventually I started to go out with other girls my age. I noticed when some of the girls got the interest of the boys, and after a while, some of the boys started noticing me. At first it made me feel uncomfortable, but then I started to talk to them. Slowly my behavior changed; I went from isolating myself and hating boys into spending time with friends and being sexually promiscuous. This was such a drastic change in myself and my behavior I hardly knew what was happening to me. I say this because I became a person even I couldn't comprehend. For example, I changed how I dressed. I started off dressing strangely, wearing several shirts at a time to hide my body, even though back then I didn't know I was doing it. Eventually, though, I went out wearing almost no clothes. I didn't really feel like this was a problem at the time, but obviously I had not dealt with the psychological emotions that often come along with incest; I went from feeling shame about my body to trying to use it, to prove I was in charge of it.

For many years my moods remained unbalanced, yet not many people knew this. Many teenagers go through a period where they rebel and lash out against their parents. I never got that opportunity as a teenager because my family had split up. I had feelings of rage and resentment against both of my parents for the parts they played in breaking up our happy home, but I never verbalized them. I did see my mother on occasion, and I have to say that it was hard to keep quiet. I sometimes wonder, if I had said something, would my mother have been able to snap her life back into what it was when she was happy? Now I'm not so naïve as to think that I had control of my mother's life, but I do think that she cared about doing what was best for my brother and me. When I didn't feel strong enough to speak about what was on my mind, I was overcome with shame. For as long as I can remember I couldn't even say the word "sex." Not only had my self-esteem suffered, but in looking back, I feel like I was robbed of many years of happiness as a child.

On the Upward Swing

It took me several years to come to terms with what happened to me as a girl, so I knew that trying to put it behind me would take some time as well. I decided that changes were in order. The process of turning my life around was far from easy; many, many years went by before I got to this point. It was a process of deciding whether I wanted to live in the past and give this tragedy the power of controlling the rest of my life, or to accept the facts of what happened and try to move on from there. I chose the latter.

To those who have not been a victim of incest, the decision may sound as though it's an easy one, but a victim can make that choice only when they're ready to work on their own path of road to resurrection. Now that I had made the decision, I had to figure out how I was going to move on. The first and most important thing I knew I had to work on was my image. I believed that image was the most important because it's the first thing people see and the last thing they remember about you when you leave. Each day when you wake up, the first thing you see in the mirror is an image of yourself. When I looked at myself, I hated what I saw, and I always thought others hated what they saw when they looked at me too. Incest can distort a person's self-image. Each morning when I got up, my mind told me that I was an ugly, fat, nasty person. Before I could move on with my life I had to confront what I saw in the mirror and what I'd heard in the back of my mind.

As a loner teenager I'd often heard about facing a challenge, so when I started saying it to myself I eventually started to believe it. I made the decision to work on me as my challenge. I began by changing the way I referred to myself; each day I started by telling myself one thing I liked about myself. When my mind reverted to my negative thoughts, I wrote down goals I'd accomplished over the last sixmonths. I knew that if I wanted others to see how happy and content I was, I had to be happy with myself first. I also set out to buy clothes that made me feel good. Clothing alone doesn't change a person, but it definitely can provide a fresher and more confident look.

My outside image was getting pretty close to where I wanted it to be, so now I had to work on believing it in my mind and in my heart. This was my biggest challenge. Many people have different weaknesses; mine was my low self-esteem. I sought help in many ways. First, I fell in love with a wonderful man during my high school years. We stayed together for many years, and built a lasting relationship, even having a child together. Having a baby was a new experience for me; it allowed me to experience such a great love, unlike I've ever felt before. I was a great mother early on, and this increased my self-esteem somewhat. When my son started getting older ,I returned to college and later graduated. These two achievements made me somewhat happy for a period of time, but because I wasn't married, I felt as though something was missing. After several years of being with my son's father, we broke up. At times, I felt sad and very depressed about my failed relationship and my life—it was a very hard time in my life. Thankfully my mother was able to be there for support. I realized I had found myself at a crossroads in my life.

Be Truthful with Yourself about What You Want

Over the years I had been battling depression, and now the time had come to do something different. I loved my son, and I wanted to love life just as much. Knowing how I felt about my child and how being a good mother raised my self-esteem, I wanted to explore working with children.

I got my new start at a new job at a local agency in a nearby town that worked with at-risk families, pregnant women, and small children. I could identify with some of the family situations, and worked hard to provide information on how to assist families in making different choices. I eventually learned more about child development and even applied some of the information to raising my own son. Not only was I providing great information, but I was practicing the information I had learned. Even better, after seeing the impact on some of the young children, I knew I was in the right place, and had found my passion of working with children.

Over the years, my job gave me purpose and joy like I'd never felt before. I helped to break the cycle of domestic violence in a few families' lives; I educated mothers on the signs of incest; I assisted mothers in going back to school; and I helped to decrease the number of babies born with low birth weight. Happily, I even got a chance to be present for the births of some of those babies. I developed a greater passion for the process of birth and started to believe that birth was the beginning of many things beautiful, pure, and magical. As I delved more into the beauty of birth, it allowed me to learn more about myself. I had an epiphany: as I taught women about the joy of birth and how their lives were going to change, my own life changed, too. I realized that birth meant something special and magical to me, and that this was just the beginning of me being resurrected.

During my time at the agency, I learned so much about myself and how to move past things that had been holding me hostage for many years. It was almost as though I had woken up from a long, deep sleep. It was now time to give birth to the life that I once lost after being a victim of incest. I had no idea how I would do it, but I knew I had to start somewhere. My guilt, sadness, and fear had been holding me back for quite some time, but the time had come to face my fears. I started questioning how I would handle my fear of moving forward. I never really came to a concrete conclusion, but I went forward with the intent that I would face my fear and gain more self-confidence along the way.

Prepare Yourself to Work on Your Fears and Challanges

My first challenge was put to the test immediately. I had to go into a jail to work with a pregnant woman. I found it difficult not to be afraid. At first I approached the situation with great apprehension, but soon, with guidance and a place to discuss my fears, I was able to work through my feelings and eventually do the work. Facing and accomplishing one of my fears gave me more confidence in myself, and allowed me to open the door to facing other things that were holding me back.

I also had a crippling fear of public speaking. When I had to give a presentation, I would become physically sick or just not make an attempt at all. Eventually, I discussed my fear of public speaking with a former supervisor. Under her direction, I had picked up some tips before about how I could overcome my fear. At the time I don't think I was completely ready to commit to working on it, but the more I practiced, I did it the more comfortable I became. When I stopped resisting and tried to work through my fear of speaking in public, to my surprise it became much easier—who knew!

Working on improving my image and getting my voice back felt almost as though I were being born again. Finally, I felt like I was ready to find love again too.

KEEP AN OPEN MIND TO THE UNKNOWN

It had been a few years since my son's father and I had separated, and I had been through the process of resurrecting myself. I met someone special; he walked into my life when I was trying to rebuild it. Ironically, when I first met him I didn't think that it would last because he was egotistical and a little overbearing—not the typical guy I usually dated. After I really got to know him, though, he turned out to be a great friend, and now a person who I care very much for.

The early stages of our getting to know each other were rocky, as I believe we both had a lot of work to work on in our separate lives. Luckily for him, he came in during the last stages of me resurrecting myself. Curtis appeared to be in the midst of a storm in his own life, and I wasn't sure whether I wanted to go down this path with someone else after just having come full circle on my own. But I made the decision to stay with him. I eventually introduced Curtis to my son, Jaden, and after we had dated for a while he moved in with us. I didn't know if it was the right thing to do without being married, but the only way to know was to take a chance.

Curtis and I continued to live together for a while, but we were more friends than lovers. I become involved with a man named Darrell. I really didn't know which man was right for me, and things were complicated. Eventually, Darrell moved to another state, and I realized I missed his presence. Since the move Darrell and I have been in a long-distance relationship. For now, I'm not sure where we will end up, but I know that I appreciate Curtis' support and encouragement along the way.

Surround Yourself with Positive People and Influences

My mother has also been a great support for me. Over the years, the incest and the drugs really affected the bond between my mother and me, and we have a difficult relationship at times because of the past. Sometimes we speak, and other times we don't. I never really understand why we have such inconsistency in our relationship now, but I know that when I need her she will be there and that she knows she can expect the same from me. With the support of friends and family, and a new outlook on life, I know that I am in a place where I can move forward.

Call Upon a Higher Power

I have a deep relationship with my faith. Whenever I feel lost or sad, I know that God is always there to listen and help me work through any problems that may arise. I believe that anyone who has ever experienced incest will find the right path, whether he or she believes in a higher power or not. For me, it's important to know that God is always there to listen, but even so, I knew that my faith alone could not be everything.

Having had a personal relationship with a higher power throughout my process of resurrection is the reason I feel that I must share my story. My God has taken care of me and my family during this whole process, and he will be able to take care of anyone else who is going through anything. My hope for my future is to continue on my resurrecting path, to stay grounded with God, and to develop a closer personal relationship with him and to trust where God is leading me in my life. I would never want to come across as preaching, but I know how a belief in the higher power has worked in my life, and I know that if anyone else experiencing incest or molestation called upon whatever higher power that he or she believed in, I know that it will work in the same way in his or her life, too.

Seek the Support of the Community and Designated Officials

Not everyone is open to the idea of getting professional counseling to work through major issues in their lives; some feel that family and childhood issues should be kept private and shared only within family. I believe a person has the right to choose what is best for him- or herself. I kept the incest private because I felt guilty, ashamed, ugly, and powerless. I not only felt like it was the most awful thing to have happened, but also hated myself for splitting up my family. If I had seen a professional, maybe the incest would have stopped sooner, and maybe the effects would not have gone on for so long in my life. As an adult now, I ask myself why I never told a teacher, or why I never left home. I can't answer any of those questions. What I do know is that now I'm in my thirties and I have decided to talk about how this incest has shaped me into the person that I have come to be, if for no other reason than I want to prevent someone else from being in the same situation I find myself in. Now that I'm at a place where I'm ready to accept and discuss what happened, I can finally open the door to working with a professional. With the hope of accepting the past and moving forward, I want to help other people find their own path to resurrection. When a person has come to the place that he or she is ready to accept the inevitable fallout of having been a victim of incest, and is ready to move on from there, he or she will know that he will be ready to start his own path to resurrection.

I will never be able to go back and change the fact that I was molested, but I can continue on my path to rebuilding my life into what I want it to be today. It is my hope that one day I can be an inspiration to others suffering incest or molestation; I want my story to inspire them to feel like they have the power over their attackers. It is my hope that a younger child can get up the strength to speak up sooner rather than later about the incest or molestation, regardless if the incest is being done by a family member or by someone in school.

To build the bridge from home life to school, I hope some form of annual training, perhaps mandated by law, could be put into place in our New York schools that teaches teachers to be more skilled in recognizing the signs of sexual abuse. After parents, teachers are the people who see children the most; they really get to know what's normal for each student. I remember one particular teacher taking a great interest in me in my first year of high school; I believe she knew something was happening at home, only she may not have known how to broach the subject.

One thing to keep in mind when dealing with children is that all students are different. Some students are very open and communicate well, while others are very shy. The shy ones would never openly discuss anything out of the ordinary unless someone asks them the right questions. I know that if my teacher had sat me down and asked me direct questions about being touched at home, I wouldn't have been able to discuss that with her. As a shy person, I needed someone to ask me how I was doing, but in the right way; because it never happened, I allowed the molestation to continue much longer than it should have. Children rely on adults to take care of them and to look out for their well-being. It's possible that had an adult asked me questions, and I had found a way to talk about my abuse, I may have been able to move on much earlier.

Still, I am on a path to changing myself and my life. First, I hope to continue improving upon my image. I had lack of interest in my self-image after the incest, but I began to turn that around with positive speech and an outward makeover. Continuing on my resurrecting path, I would like to take this even further in my life and address the issues I have with my weight. I want to live a healthier lifestyle going forward. It's important to me to really attempt to feel good about myself in every way possible.

Another important piece of the puzzle to me was a healthier attitude. After the incest my self-esteem had really taken a dive, as I previously mentioned. Now that I've started turning my life around, I've overcome shame, guilt, and many of the fears that kept me from moving on in my life in my earlier years. I set out to raise my self-esteem in many ways. First, I built a lasting relationship with my son by being the best mother

I could be. Then I went back to college and worked to help others. After building on these things, I decided that I wanted to work on things on a more personal level. I challenged myself to look inside; although it wasn't easy, it was necessary to help me become a happier person from the inside out. Anyone going through his or her own process of resurrection knows that this is not an easy task, but it is the first step to rebuilding one's life, which certainly helps to raise self-esteem and create a more hopeful outlook. One great way to get on this path is to dedicate some time to think about doing some things that once made you happy.

Take Time Out for Yourself

Doing things for yourself is important in the process of resurrecting yourself. If you don't take an interest in yourself, no one else will either. Sometimes we can get caught up in other peoples' lives and forget about doing what makes us happy. Coming from a person who has put her needs and happiness last, it's important to never forget about what makes you happy! A person who has taken care of everyone else often doesn't have the energy to take care of himself; this is when depression and sadness creeps back. I was told never to allow myself to get so wrapped up in the lives of others that I didn't have time to find happiness in my own life. My hope is to always be aware of this. I'm always open to helping others, but it's important for me to never forget about myself in the process. It is my hope that others put this into practice as well.

Doing what makes you happy will be different for everyone. You may already know some things that make you happy. For me happiness comes in many forms. Some of the simplest things make me happy: seeing my son Jaden leave each day for school with a smile on his face, for example. To some this may sound cliché, but when I was his age, it was very hard for me to smile. It gives me joy to see happiness in my child's face. Another thing that makes me happy is being able to discuss my past and the incest without feeling shame anymore. Having a relationship with Curtis makes me happy too. He has been a support and good friend during this whole process.

I look back to where I was ten years ago and I see how far I have come after this whole process. Working on myself has been a long, drawn-out ordeal, but after a lot of work I can smile with genuine joy from the inside out, and to me that's priceless. Starting out as a person with many trust issues and a distorted image of what a loving relationship should be, I've grown into a woman who has opened her heart to finding love and the possibility of happiness with the right man. Along the way I've allowed myself to start to trust.

Be creative and don't limit yourself to saying that you'll never do something. I love to write, and that's why I decided to write this book. At first it started out as a journal of my private thoughts. After about six pages or so, the idea of the book was born. I also take great joy in cooking new and unfamiliar foods. I've found that cooking seems to be very relaxing for me, so perhaps that's why I like it so much. Perhaps I'll write a book with family recipes! When I'm cooking, I find myself remembering some of the foods that I grew up on, and it takes me back to happier times and good family moments.

Live One Day at a Time

I try to live one day at a time. I find that taking on too much can bring overwhelming stress with it. This approach may not work for everyone, but each person will know what works best for them. I hope to live one day at a time and to enjoy each day as if it were my last. In other words, if there's something that you want to do or a place you've wanted to go, put it on the list of things that you're going to do for yourself during your own road to resurrection. Personally, I've always wanted to write a book, but I've never had that much to say about one topic before now, nor did I ever have the courage. How about that self-esteem, huh?

As a person going through a process of resurrection in your life, you will feel or think of something that you've always wanted to do or say, and that will be something you will do along your own path of resurrection. My only hope is that your moment will come sooner rather than later, for you owe it to yourself to be the best you can be possibly be. If you feel like you might need guidance, seek help from a higher power; look to your faith to help you through the tough times.

Leaving the Past Behind

Moving forward starts with looking ahead, not back to where you were. I find that many people who have been the victim of incest have trouble looking ahead because they haven't yet dealt with their past. It is not for me to say that their roads will be easy—mine certainly wasn't—but when one is ready to start on one's own road to resurrection, the time and effort will prove well worth it. At the end of the path, the traveler will have come full circle and will have positioned him- or herself for a better and even brighter future. We are not defined by our past; we can be ready for what's in store for our much-anticipated future.

Printed in the United States
By Bookmasters